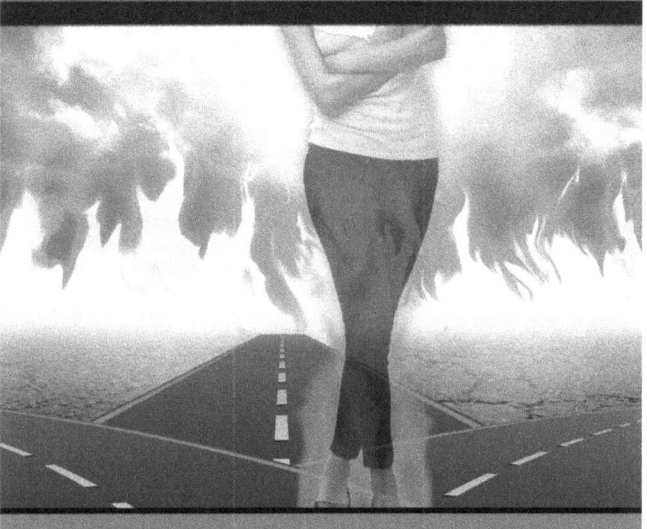

THROUGH THE FIRE

Mechelle Bailey

THROUGH THE FIRE

Mechelle Bailey

Mechelle Bailey
Through the Fire

© 2016, Mechelle Bailey
Anointed Fire™ House
(mskingdomjewel@gmail.com)

ALL RIGHTS RESERVED. This book contains material protected under International and Federal Copyright Laws and Treaties. Any unauthorized reprint or use of this material is prohibited. No part of this book may be reproduced or transmitted in any form or by any means, electronic or mechanical, including photocopying, recording, or by any information storage and retrieval system without express written permission from the author/publisher.

I have tried to recreate events, locales and conversations from my memories of them. In order to maintain their anonymity in some instances I have changed the names of individuals and places, I may have changed some identifying characteristics and details such as physical properties, occupations and places of residence.

ISBN-13: 978-0692660324
ISBN-10: 0692660321

Acknowledgments

- First and foremost, I cannot give any accolades or acknowledgments without giving all thanks to God, who covered and guided me through the fire. I will be forever grateful for the kingdom connections that God orchestrated for this book to be birthed.

- I am grateful for the mentorship and Remnant Writers Institute for the push in releasing this overdue baby. If it had not been for Tiffany Buckner and my other accountability partners, this book would have remained overdue. I thank you, Tiffany, for the seasoned prophetic scribe in you being assigned to my birthing room.

- I am grateful for my children and family who prayed for me during my darkest seasons. Lastly, I am forever thankful for the God sisters who have waited patiently for this book to be released, encouraging, pushing, and reminding me of the countless women who are in need of the testimony I have humbly laid out in the pages of this book.

Table of Contents

Introduction..IX

Chapter 1..
  Lying in the Lap of Delilah..............................1

Chapter 2..
  Letter & Message to the Other Woman. 25

Chapter 3..
  Divine Restoration..35

Chapter 4..
  Hell Hounds Unleashed..................................43

Chapter 5..
  Love Homework: Signs of a Wounded Woman..61

Chapter 6..
  Love Homework; Double Trouble...............67

Chapter 7..
  The Company We Keep..................................83

Chapter 8..
  In the Ninth Hour...95

Chapter 9..
  Through the Fire...101

Introduction

As I began to look back over the last ten years of my life, I wrestled with my story. I had to realize that it is a familiar story for every woman who has had an adulterous spouse. It is a familiar story for every woman who has encountered counterfeits... from the hell hounds she's dated to the company she's kept. Friendly fire from inside is more damaging than a known enemy on the outside. When God began to heal and restore me, I came to realize that even though my story may be familiar to many, every woman has not been equipped, anointed, and appointed to write the story. *Through the Fire* is my story laid out for all to know. It details how, in the midst of the fire, the Lord provided strategies and reinforcement to assist me in the fiery furnaces of refinement. My redemption through the blood of Jesus guided me through that refinement. Going through the fire taught me how to not only trust God, but to lean into the very essence of God to survive in the fire.

Chapter 1
<u>Lying in the Lap of Delilah</u>

I am writing this book as the Spirit of God moves upon me to release this message. We have all experienced many trials and circumstances in our lives that made us question if God was for us or against us. During my trials, I suffered the loss of two children through miscarriage and I also endured the reality of three children being born into my marital union, but not of my womb. During these ordeals, the Lord continued to tell me that my steps were being ordered by Him. He also said He'd given my husband a window of grace to repent for his sins. After all these traumas came the unexpected death of my husband in 2008. He had been my high school sweetheart and the father of my (children). To add insult to injury, he'd been killed inside of an apartment he'd just moved into with his girlfriend of seven months.

My phases of grief were very unstable. I listened to the voice of God and separated from my husband after the second Ishmael was conceived. God ministered to me and reminded me that there is therefore now no condemnation to them which are in are in Christ Jesus, who walk not after the flesh, but after the spirit." (Romans 8:1, KJV).

"The steps of a [good] man are directed and established by the Lord when He delights in his way and He busies Himself with his every step" (Psalms 37:23, Amp).

Through it all, my steps were being ordered to walk in the mantle that God had predestined for me to walk in before the foundations of the world. This was a journey I'd been assigned to before my mother knew my father. Nothing in God happens without Him allowing it to happen. Was my husband saved? Yes, he was. Sometimes, our wanting to please others, unresolved generational curses, and refusing to surrender the Lord prevents us from allowing our steps to be ordered.

My husband wrestled and overcame the temptation to commit adultery many times, but without God, he wasn't strong enough to win that battle. When we continue to toy with sin, it will keep us longer than we want to stay in it, take us further than we want to go in it, and cost us more than we want to pay for it.
"When lust hast conceived, it brings forth sin, and sin when it is finished, brings forth death"(James 1:15, KJV).

It hurt me to my core to write this because when you love someone as deep as I loved my husband, you do not want them to be caught with their pants down or their oil lamp unlit. We (my children and I) do believe that in his ninth hour, he called out to his Father God to save him and he repented of his sins. So, in my closing, I must reiterate that many situations in our lives are God ordered; especially when He has preordained the steps we are to take. I summon everyone who reads this book to take a spiritual inventory of your life and make sure that the steps you are walking in are God ordered and not God allowed. What a difference!!!!

I appeal to those of you who have allowed friends and family to dictate which steps you are to take. I challenge you to take that power back and give it to God, for in the Spirit of God is liberty. Make sure the steps you are taking are in Him and not man. God has warned us many times to put our trust in no man. Such as the case with my husband; God warned him many times through his spiritual father and various other vessels of God to stop his philandering and return to God. They even warned the family God had assigned to him. It's a dangerous thing to be outside of your assigned house of God (marriage covenant). When you are not God led, you are leading yourself, and being self-led will sometimes take you into trenches not authorized by God. I write this book to help those who are in a situation that you know isn't of God, and I write also to plead with those who have turned a deaf ear to the Lord. I appeal to you to repent, get delivered and recover your purpose in God.

I write to the women who have been where I've been and the women who are still there. I write to you, asking that you loose yourself from the yoke of bondage.

Lying in the Lap of Delilah
(Unexpected End)
Who Are You Connected To?

When Samson fell for a woman named Delilah, he did not know that it would cost him his life. She was the mark of the beginning of his downfall. You have to be careful who you invite into your intimate chambers because they could be from the devil.

Delilah was a woman from the valley of Sorek. The Philistine's leaders collaborated with Delilah and offered her money to find out the secrets to Samson's strength. Be careful who you reveal your secrets to, because they might use them against you.

While Samson was sleeping on Delilah's lap, she called in a co-conspirator to shave off his seven braids, and then, he subdued him because he had become weak. You have to protect your anointing, and protect your heart; be careful who you give your heart to.

As I lie on my bed overwhelmed with grief over the loss of my husband, I tried to wrap my mind around what had transpired. I silently asked the Lord from within my heart, "What happened to him?" God began to reveal to me that he'd laid his head on the lap of Delilah, an unassigned woman who was sent to gain entrance into his spirit and deliver him into the hands of his enemies.

I asked the Lord what the word "Delilah" meant, and He began to reveal to me that "Delilah" means a seductive and treacherous woman. This revelation shook me. The Lord also told me that my husband had crossed over outside of his covering (marital vows) and his vow unto the Lord. My husband's appetite for the accursed things grew beyond his comprehension, even though God had delivered him many times from those curses. On the day of my husband's death, the Lord gave me a dream. In the dream, I saw my husband and he kept asking me to come and get him, but I kept asking him about the woman he was currently living with. After all, she was pregnant with his child. In the dream, he kept saying that she was on her own and that she'd done it (gotten pregnant) to herself. I truly didn't understand what he was trying to tell me because I was so clouded by the fact that he had impregnated another woman, adding to the fold of outside children and bringing the number to three. In the dream, he kept begging me to come and get him. Finally, I humbled myself and told him I would. When I pulled up to his residence, he ran out to my car. That's when I saw her. She covered herself with a black coat and disappeared into another car. Once he was inside the car, he asked me to forgive him, and he told me that he loved me.

He asked if I would take him to work, and of course, I agreed. I still haven't received the full understanding of this dream and what was being spoken to me. A few people have tried to interpret this dream, but whenever I take their interpretations before the Lord, He reveals that their interpretations are off. I desperately wanted to release this dream to my husband the day of his unexpected end. We'd spoken a few times that morning, and I wanted to warn him, but the Lord would not bring the dream back to my remembrance. I have often asked the Lord why He would not allow me to release my dream to my husband that morning, but all I seem to get is silence. His silence seems to override the voice within me, quieting my spirit and urging me to simply trust in the Lord. You must ask yourself who you are connected to. Many times people are not who they appear to be.

Here are some questions you must ask as you connect yourself:

1). Is he or she consistent in their interactions with you? Many times we dismiss those little hiccups as a person having a bad day, or we are so preoccupied with the presenter that we miss what's actually being presented.

2). Have you been able to observe all the seasons with this person? Just as there are four seasons in a year, the character of people changes to reveal the many facets of their personalities. Their seasons reveal how they handle circumstances in their lives as well.

3). Have you done your research on the generational curses of divorce, separation, and adultery within the family lineage? Many times, things don't manifest in an individual until that person has fulfilled the assignment of locking you into a committed relationship.

Every woman wants to believe that infidelity couldn't happen to her. Many women continuously walk around in denial until infidelity comes to full bloom in their lives. Every time my husband cheated, I wrestled with not wanting to be a statistic and I took on the load of trying to save the marriage myself. However, God showed me that He was and is the first husband in my life. He continued to provide for my children and I while my husband bounced between going to jail and the bedrooms of other women. My reality hit me like a ton of bricks as I mentally replayed the last nineteen years of my life. I grasped at every possible line of reasoning I could find to numb the pain when it surfaced.

One day, the Lord woke me up to tell me that

the spirit that possessed my husband has been in his family's bloodline for years. Every time he went back on his promises to God and me, those spirits became stronger within him.

The word of Lord says, "Then the lust, when it hath conceived, beareth sin: and the sin, when it is fullgrown, bringeth forth death" (James 1:15, ASV). My husband was an ordained Minister and knew the Bible, yet he still battled with the spirits of lust, adultery, and covetousness.

There were times when I would tell him to just wait on the Lord to bless us with certain things, but because he saw others get material possessions with fast money, he continued to go back to the enemy's camp and play Russian roulette with his soul. He would come home and beg me not to leave him on many occasions. He would ask me to pray for him, and I would pray fervently to the Lord on his behalf. Things seemed to change temporarily, but that root would always spring back up with greater intensity.

The gifts he had inside him were amazing. He had the gift to bring revelation and insight of the Word of God. He also had a teaching gift that could bring children to salvation. I witnessed victories in his life when he allowed God to have full control of him. The powerful prayers he would pray over our children and others within the ministry were amazing.

The story of Samson and Delilah brought such a revelation to me that I was able to come out of the shame, grief, and guilt I had for not being able to warn him of his unexpected end. Even in the midst of the pain he'd inflicted on me through his infidelities and pride, I didn't want to see him fail at fulfilling the great purpose I knew he had on his life.

Sometimes, we can see the greatness in others that they cannot seem to see in themselves. Just like Samson, he had such an anointing upon his life that he continued to go into the enemy's camp, thinking that he wouldn't be overcome.

Needless to say, Delilah was assigned to subdue my husband so that he would be taken over by the Philistines. The spirit of Delilah continues to operate in many today, and not just women, but it also operates in men. The spirit of Delilah has a deceiving heart designed to seduce people. On one hand, the Delilah spirit speaks sweet words to gain someone's trust, but then, it will turn around and commit evil with its other hand.

How many of us know of someone with these exact characteristics? How many times have we ignored the red flags because we were so absorbed in the seduction of the forbidden fruits that were being used to entice us away from our purposes? The red flags are present, and that's why it is very important to have discernment. You need to know when you are in the presence of a Delilah spirit. If the person you are connected to or being pursued by constantly tries to suffocate your time and is always telling you that everyone else is against you, you are involved with a spirit of Delilah.

The Delilah spirit thrives off control and manipulation in order to lock down its prey. A Delilah spirit will utilize false emotions in an attempt to make its prey feel as if it has their best interests at heart. In reality, it is weaving a web of deception designed to assassinate its prey. Delilah feeds off the purpose and untapped anointing of the individual it is assigned to destroy. If you have encountered this spirit, you must know that the purpose that is living within you is greater than you can imagine. The kingdom of hell wouldn't assign such a vicious assassin to take you out spiritually, mentally, and emotionally if it didn't see you as a threat.

Many times in our lives, we had to die to our own agendas, motives and ambitions to allow the Lord to have complete control. Life without God isn't life at all. God has a way of bringing things to pass, and the only requirement is for us to surrender our hearts, minds and souls to Him. God will not allow His children to be ignorant of the enemy's devices, but when we continue to ignore the warning signs, labels, and tables, we frustrate the paths that God has set to bring us a bright future.

"For I know the plans I have for you," says the LORD. "They are plans for good and not for disaster, to give you a future and a hope

(Jeremiah 29:11, NLT).

Many people have prematurely left the earth without fulfilling any of the assignments that were assigned to them by God. The Lord desires to see His children prosper and not fail in anything that He has equipped them to win in. When a marriage dies without the purpose of that covenant union being fulfilled, it upsets God. It also upsets God to see family members and so-called friends accept the brokenness of the covenant. In some family dynamics, infidelity is a common practice. I learned this from experience the first time I called my husband's mother about his wayward ways. She firmly told me, in so many words, his behavior was normal, especially for the men born in his family.

I couldn't believe what I was hearing. His mother basically told me to stop crying and be happy because I had the ring. What about the fact that I wanted the vows that were made with the ring as well? She went on to tell me that his father had cheated on her.

I learned to prepare my heart for the seasons when my husband would stray outside of our marriage. I began to almost pinpoint the very hour that he'd become entangled in his affairs. Many would argue that the Lord wouldn't warn, lead or reveal to me my husband's weaknesses for other women, but this is not true. According to His Word, "*Surely the Lord God will do nothing, but he revealeth his secret unto his servants the prophets*" (Amos 3:7, KJV).

The Lord never allowed me to be ignorant of my husband's extracurricular activities. There were times when my emotions would get the best of me. There were many times I would go into my bedroom, ball up into the fetal position,

and cry uncontrollably. I did this because I didn't want my children to witness my brokenness. My husband would always come home, and with tears in his eyes, he'd beg me not to leave him. He would even go to church, ask for prayer while at church, and he would appear to be walking in his deliverance.
I came to realize that those spirits were lying dormant in him. They deceived me to gain access back into my heart. I will admit that there was a time when my husband walked heavy in his deliverance and maintained a monogamous lifestyle. I must also confess that those were the times when our marriage was at a heightened state within the spiritual realm, and we would spend hours praying and working in the ministry.

My husband was active within our church and the men loved his charisma. There were so many times when I had to suffer in silence, even within my church. There were many people battling lust and sexual perversion in our church at that time, and many of them remained active in leadership without any consequences for their indiscretions.

My husband and I went to counseling at the church, but the finger of blame was always pointed at me. I was often asked what I'd done to make him stray. These type of interrogations wreaked havoc on my spirit. My self-esteem was shattered and I constantly told myself to leave, move forward and never look back. Many people from my church constantly used the Bible to badger me, saying I needed to be a more submissive wife, mother, and woman of God.

One day, I prayed out of the abundance of my brokenness, and all of sudden, peace came over me. I began to allow the Lord to quiet my spirit and I stopped fighting to save a marriage that had been broken by numerous adulterous affairs.

My husband's appetite for other women grew to the point where I began to receive prophetic messages in dreams, from prophets, and from one of our children. I became very scared of what my husband's final outcome would be, never considering for one minute that he wouldn't be here in the natural to assist in raising his kids.

My prayers became less about restoration and more about forgiveness and releasing the marriage. My heart, at that time, couldn't comprehend death. My heart, at that time, couldn't comprehend the idea that I'd never have a happily ever after with him. However, my spirit became grieved even before his death. The last time I saw my husband physically, I wept because it was evident that the physical connection between us was dissipating.

When he hugged me the last time we were in each other's presence, his spirit cried out for me to help him, but his natural body remained in bondage. When he drove away, my spirit began to weep. I grieved because I couldn't rescue him from the iniquities that were consuming him. He looked so different from the man I'd once fallen in love with. Sin has a way of changing a person's appearance and molding them to reveal the stage it is currently in.

In the Bible, the Word of the Lord reveals the phases of sin and its outcome when it is at its fullness. Have you ever seen a person in their innocence before life takes its toll on them? A person's countenance is very bright and flawless until they begin to experience sin. Sin will take a beautiful young woman and age her by twenty years. Sin is an ancient spirit that has been on this earth for thousands of years. Sin is no respecter of person and holds no loyalty to the many marital covenants it has broken. Sin has no conviction for the many lives it has destroyed.

"So put to death the sinful, earthly things lurking within you. Have nothing to do with sexual immorality, impurity, lust, and evil desires. Don't be greedy, for a greedy person is an idolater, worshiping the things of this world. Because of these sins, the anger of God is coming" (Colossians 3:5-6, NLT).

The Word of the Lord clearly tells us to put to death sin and its inner workings from within us. When generational sins are not renounced and dealt with it, they can have a profound effect on the life of the individual who is enslaved to sin. Be prayerful and seek the Lord about habitual and generational sins in the bloodline.

Chapter 2
Letter & Message to the Other Woman

The Letter

One year, on my husband's birthday, I stumbled across a message from one of his many women. She was writing a shout out to him as if they shared a healthy and committed relationship. This really disturbed me, and even though I didn't normally address my husband's mistresses, I felt the need to confront her. Somehow, boldness rose up within me and I began to write a letter to the woman who felt she had the right to post pictures, profess her love and give a shout out to my husband. Many would say I should have ignored it and she had a right to display her feelings to him in the company of her own audience, but some of those who were her audience were our family members and mutual friends. I felt a strong release within my spirit to write it out and address this issue. I felt like Hannah, grieved within my spirit and forgotten by God of the promises. I prayed before the Lord, and with my pen in my hand, I began to pour out on paper what was in my heart.

The Letter to the Other Woman.

I tried to keep my thoughts private, but it seems to keep surfacing. When you are the other woman, sideline or whatever your title may be, you don't have the same posture and position of a wife. Today is serious to my family, and it may be to you too, but God doesn't even recognize you, so why should anyone else? It makes me mad when the playmates who laid and played outside my marriage continue to try to counterfeit my position as a wife. As the wife, I have the rights and authority to publicly post pictures and whatever I want to post. Your memories don't even compare to 19 years, not one bit. So, if you have some decency or fear of God in you, remain in the position you were left in and stop trying to build a story on grounds already appointed. It's called marriage, not adultery! God's Word still stands. Ishmael can never obtain an Isaac blessing! This day it's called bootlegging; it's not the real thing.

Now, allow me to educate you on what your position really was, and I pray that once you come into the knowledge of the truth, you will take the necessary steps to get free of being this type of woman. All throughout history, your type has been around... even back in biblical times. In the bible, you are known as a "<u>concubine</u>." A concubine, in the bible, is a woman who lives or cohabits with a man without being married to him. She is a secondary wife; one having a recognized social status in a household below that of a wife. A concubine, as laid out in today's terminology, is a mistress, servant, slave, surrogate mother and a sex partner. Historically, many of you were hired to fulfill appetites bigger than my husband could handle. A lot of times during our separation, he came to his assigned house for peace. He needed refuge away from the chaos he created with you while operating in the lusts of his flesh. When he would walk through the door, I could name who he had been with because in the spirit realm, the Lord color coded all of you for me to identify. For example, one of you was green (full of wickedness and jealousy) another blue (flesh and lust)... just to name a few. I dreamed of your various assignments on him many times, but there was a season where the Lord told me to be silent... no more warnings. He didn't just have one of you against me; he had a harem of you. As a concubine, you become an <u>odalisque:</u> a woman slave in a harem. So, to serve you notice, I was never the competition or a threat. I didn't need to compete or come out of position. My position was anointed and appointed by God under the contract of marital covenant. The devil has tricked many of you out of wholesome relationships with men who were available to enter into covenants with you. Instead, it seemed more exciting for you to play a part in coming against God's covenant. "*Marriage is honorable in all, and the bed undefiled; but whoremongers and adulterers God will judge*" (Hebrews 13:4, KJV).

Many of you grew up in families where it was the norm for the women to have relationships with other women's husbands and not think anything of it. Many of you will never apologize or come to the realization of who you really were in his life. Family and friends may sugar coat the lies for you and tell you that he wasn't happy at home, I wasn't doing my job, and a list of other lies. I suffered a miscarriage in the heat of all of his affairs, and for a long time, I was hurt as to why the child conceived within my marital covenant wasn't able to be born. Since that time, God has given me some clarity and revelation.

The spirit of the concubine will continue to enslave you until you truly deal with the essence of you being a mistress, a counterfeit and a harlot. The Word of the Lord speaks, *"Therefore now, hear this, you who love pleasures and are given over to them, you who dwell safely and sit securely, who say in your mind, I am (the mistress) and there is no one else besides me. I shall not sit as a widow, nor shall I know the loss of children."*
"For you, (Babylon) have trusted your

wickedness; you have said, No one sees me. Your wisdom and your knowledge led you astray, and you said in your heart and mind, I am, and there is no one besides me. Therefore, shall evil come upon you" (Isaiah 47:8, 10-11, amplified).

As a mistress, you are engrossed in compromise where you may receive compensation for your services. This falls under a different title: prostitute. The book of Proverbs describes you perfectly and clearly. *"With her enticing speech she caused him to yield, with her flattering lips she seduced him. Immediately he went after her, as an ox goes to the slaughter, Or as a fool to the correction of the stocks, till an arrow struck his liver. As a bird hastens to the snare, He did not know it would cost his life. Now therefore, listen to me, my children; pay attention to the words of my mouth: Do not let your heart turn aside to her ways. Do not stray into her paths; for she has cast down many wounded, and all who were slain by her were strong men. Her house is the way to hell, descending to the chambers of death" (Proverbs 7:21-27).*

The relationship built between you two was solely based on sex and money. A man already in covenant with a wife cannot be any more than a borrowed piece of man in your life, offering you a temporary means of pleasure. A man in bondage to lust can only speak to you from the lustful stream rising from within the heat of his loins, not from the chambers of his heart. When he was really knee deep in torment, it was my lap he laid on, trying to figure out how he ended up in the positions he'd found himself in. When you are the assigned woman in a man's life, meaning, his "wife", there is a place within his heart, mind, and soul that could be soothed through your prayers. You will never be able to fulfill this as an unauthorized and illegal concubine.

Reflection Questions

- Have you counted up the cost of being a <u>concubine</u>?

- Have you ever been in a healthy committed relationship?

- If you could reevaluate your position in a married man's life, would you still allow yourself to be hired?

- What was your emotional and spiritual foundation prior to becoming involved with someone else's husband?

- Now that you know the consequences your position will have in your life, do you still want to remain in the relationship? Have you repented for your lifestyle?

Chapter 3
<u>Divine Restoration</u>

Soul Cry As I Rehearse Lie after Lie

Life with you seemed like a fairy tale until one day the realization of our situation became real
When the unresolved issues between us became suspended in time
I tried to recover from this fatality
But my mind seems to be consumed with this open reality
My soul is shattered as I can no longer ask myself, "What's the matter?"
Nineteen years of loving you, wanting you and needing you, only to be left with broken pieces that continually have the ability to haunt me from century to century….
I scream out unto God: How I can recapture the years, the stolen moments, the broken

promises...
Vows we made, but other relationships you paved, on a path of being untrue....
I sought the Lord for a divine restoration from you...
~The End

After this unexpected end, I needed a place to recover, this situation ripped my spirit and soul into pieces, even though my husband and I had been separated for nine months. During this time, I tried to self-medicate with alcohol to soothe the pain lodged within me. I watched my children grieve the loss of their father, and their grief sent even greater waves of despair through me. I was powerless to ease their pain, and as a mother, being unable to help them grieved my spirit even more.

One day, two of my brothers in the Lord called me and both spoke exactly the same comforting words into my spirit. After those two conversations and spiritual warfare prayers, I began to shed the sorrow, grief, and shame. I began to get direction from the Lord to move to another state to help my children recover. One morning, I packed up all of our stuff and donated what I couldn't pack to charity, and I began to prepare for our move to another state. I knew it had to be the Lord because I drove myself and my children to Virginia, where we resided for ninety days.

In Virginia, the Lord led me to the most anointed and spirit-filled church. In this church, the Lord gave the shepherds of the house precise instructions as to what they were to do for our family. They poured into us spiritually, emotionally and naturally.

My children and I went through a series of family counseling sessions that included inner healing and deliverance. The Lord met our needs supernaturally, and we never wanted for anything. After getting comfortable and settled, the Lord instructed me to move again. I didn't question the leading of the Lord, but I should have gotten the fullness of His instructions because we ended up spending time in a city that wasn't appointed for us. Thankfully, God's grace and mercy allowed me to enjoy it briefly. I connected with many people I believed were assigned to come into our lives at that particular season. During this time, the Lord continued to allow Prophets and Apostles to speak into my life concerning His plans for me. I didn't know He was refining me for a greater work in Him.

Finally, we settled down in the city God wanted us to be. We knew it was where we were supposed to be because we wept when we arrived in the city. My spirit was no longer uneasy, but settled. God once again opened doors for a place, job and new memories for us to build upon. We finally felt at home in this new land. The Lord led me to the most powerful ministry, and that ministry fed my spirit revelation upon revelation. I learned so much being a part of that ministry. I started writing to encourage and empower women to not fall into the same pitfalls, entrapment, and counterfeits that tried to destroy me.

Honestly, I longed for companionship, and that longing started overwhelming me. I didn't want to lose ground in allowing the promises of God to be fulfilled in my life. The Holy Spirit began sitting down strongly on the inside of me. I loved to hear my Apostle's insight because it bore witness with what God had been downloading in my spirit.

I never imagined that once restoration came,

the enemy would set in motion a diabolical plan to kill the mantle that God had placed upon me. My supervisor left me a birthday card with Proverbs 10:22 in it, and I now realize it was a prophetic message: **The blessing of the LORD makes a person rich, and he adds no sorrow with it** (Proverbs 10:22, NLT).

When I say this scripture hit my spirit hard, I didn't even know how profound this scripture would play out in my life. I didn't have a clue just how revelatory this scripture would be in the battle.

My supervisor continued to have an uneasy feeling in her spirit about me relocating back to Illinois. She pleaded with me not to move, but to wait for clearance from the Lord. How many of us know that when we want someone to agree with us, we can find an army to support our plans? That's just what I did. I used all types of excuses to move back, including family issues (which there were, but didn't mean I had to relocate). I had many signs that told me it was in my best interest to stay where I was and not move back.

Chapter 4
Hell Hounds Unleashed

Every girl wants to be validated, cherished and adored; it's in our nature to want a knight in shining armor, prince, king or whatever term you use to describe the "man" of your dreams. I once read a poem that said *a dream deferred isn't a dream denied*. Only when you spend time in intimacy with the King will you be able to identify the character of God (the King) in your natural king (man).

Many things block us from surrendering to God. What happens to us right on the brink of an awesome breakthrough is we get anxious and stop following the blueprints laid out for us and we ignore valuable warnings. These warnings allow us to know the signs of the enchanters, charmers and the hell hounds unleashed to overthrow us.

Enchanter: a (whisperer of a magic spell) counterfeit of confessing the word (presumption versus truth).

(Reference: elijah.org)

Charmer: (to join by means of spells, to fascinate: have fellowship with, couple together [a society] counterfeits fellowship between believers (manipulation versus love).

(Reference: elijah.org)

Hellhound: According to mythology, a **hell hound** is a demonic dog sent straight from hell to kill. Any sign of a hellhound was symbolic to imminent death.

I had my first encounter with a hellhound two weeks after I married the wrong man. I had a dream so vivid that I still remember it with clarity. I dreamed I was in the car driving with another woman of God in the car with me, and as I was driving up a long dirt road, I was distracted by a familiar face. The person was waving for me to get out of the car, so I stopped the car and got out and proceeded to walk up the dirt road. All of a sudden, two hellhounds ran up and one of them started attacking my left hand, which was the hand that had my new wedding band on it. As I looked closer, I realized the person who waved for me to get out of the car was my second husband, Willis, whom I had just married. He put his hands in his pockets as I continued to ask for his assistance, but he appeared to be connected to the dogs. I began to pray fervently and I remembered there was a young woman riding in the car with me.

The woman in the car handed me a bible and I began to pray and command the dog to loose my hand. Finally, the dog shrunk down to the size of a puppy and they both ran off. I thank God for the Holy Spirit, for He is definitely our teacher and guide.

The Lord sent a few of his servants to bring the interpretation and fullness of what this dream was revealing to me concerning Willis, my new husband. If God hadn't released the Holy Spirit to deposit the deeper things in the spirit realm to me during this time of intense warfare, I don't know where I would be. This hour of my life felt like days of torment, but to God, it was merely an hour. I couldn't believe someone so charming could turn out to be so diabolically evil.

The Lord revealed that this smooth-talking opportunist who deceived me after the death of my first husband was many characters wrapped up in one person. He was a chameleon, and he was skilled at listening to every word I spoke to mimic what I needed. I told him the various attributes I had told the Lord I wanted in a kingdom husband.

Read with your spiritual eyes intact and your discernment sharp as I share what the Lord revealed to me about this type of counterfeit.

Demonology 101
I was knocked completely out of my comfort zone, but God, through His love for me, sent in His angels to assist me in warfare against the spirits of deception, mental cruelty and sorcery. We may not know when the Lord is going to show up, but He will come in the ninth hour to endow us with power against the forces of hell. I thank Him in advance for His hands of protection upon my life.

Part Two (Inside Assassin Unmasked)
The year 2010 started out with so much heartache, betrayal, and lies. The enemy truly

unmasked himself in people I thought were truly sent from God, only to later find out that they were spiritual hit men assigned to kill the prophet in me. They were assigned to destroy my character and my faith in God. I fought the battle with the Lord on my side and His remnant of real women and men of God. I thought I would never recover, but God's recovery room is different than man's. The trial I had to go through broke many things off me. It also taught me to do my homework on folks and stop believing everything they sell out of their mouths. I truly thought I had seen and heard it all, but new levels in God breeds new devils. Just when I was about to break forth in my assignment for God, I was enticed by a enchanter(Willis), who looked like he was of God, sounded like he was of God, and acted like he was of God. The performance was grand with him during his season of entangling me into his web. This man was the perfect gentleman; he never tried to kiss me until we were married. He listened to every dream and every Rhema word I spoke as if he were on one accord with me, but when he wasn't around me, he was holding meetings with his ex-wife... an ex he claimed he never wanted to remarry or be with. Willis was back in the bed of his ex-wife before the ink dried on our marriage certificate. He would wait until I went to work, kiss me on the way out, and then, send me horrible text messages. After that, he would tell me that he doesn't want to discuss those text messages when he returned home. Before I married him, I kept having pangs in my stomach, but I dismissed the pain as me being nervous. Willis never fought fair; he even enlisted the help of people I thought were a part of my inner circle to get insight on how to attack me at different intervals.

Willis started coming home and bringing up my

first husband, who by then, had been deceased for a few years. He even began to allow his ex-wife to call and torment me to the point where I had to change my number. He would then act as if he was going to check her, but in reality, they were conspiring even more as to how to sabotage me. The Lord revealed to me that He had allowed the situation to show me just how far the enemy will go to muzzle someone. He also told me that Willis was a snake with many faces. I experienced so much shame while in this assignment because I never thought I'd be married, and then, divorced all over again. I cherished that I had only been married to one man for the greatest part of my life, but my second husband put a blemish on that endearment. I cried out to the Lord many times about my marriage, and He ministered to me that He would provide a way of escape for me. The waiting felt like years, but it was only a season of eleven months.

After that marriage, I became more cautious about my decisions, my heart and where I was in God's plans for me. God never left me nor did He forsake me during this time. The Word of the Lord came to me concerning the finality of the war I was in, and He revealed to me that I was coming out with clean hands and that I would recover everything I lost.

The Lord brought to my remembrance the dream He had given me two weeks after I'd married Willis. I dreamed of two big dogs (hell hounds), and one of them was trying to attack my marriage hand. As I was calling out to my husband to get the dog, he continued to rock back and forth on a porch while ignoring me. I remembered that the Word of the Lord came to me and commanded that the hell hound release my hand in the name of Jesus. The hell hound released my hand and shrank down to the size of a puppy, running off in the opposite direction.

After my dream about the hell hounds, the Lord continued to speak to me through dreams. I constantly dreamed of gray cats, possums, snakes and hell hounds. I began to write what the Lord was speaking to me and I continued to receive interpretations of those dreams. Nevertheless, I got really sick before I was released to file my divorce papers. I was vomiting for seven days straight.

God released a close friend of mine (who was a Prophetess) to come in as reinforcement. He also released some other very powerful warfare soldiers to pray against the darts, and evil spirits sent to attack me from this enchanter who disguised himself as my husband. They warred day and night as I was being purged of all the poisons put into me by this vile spirit. God connected me with a ministry where the Apostle prayed fervently, covering me as I warred with this spirit. God had enlisted an army of soldiers to war for my soul and my life because this spirit was literally trying to take me out.

Once the Lord freed me, the voice of the Lord told me to release Willis, and once I released him, I wouldn't have to see him or those spirits that inhabited him anymore. God severed every tie to this assigned assassin.

One day, I calculated how long I was married to my second husband, and it surprised me that it was only 11 months. Spiritually, the number 11 represents disorder: Disintegration which means a loss or serious disruption, a decaying of something.

Oh, how God loves His children! I truly had to leave the marriage to recover in God. Some days, I have flashbacks that make me sad, because I truly didn't want to be deceived this way, but who are we to pick and choose our afflictions? For the Word of God says, *"Many are the afflictions of the righteous: but the Lord delivereth him out of them all"* (Psalms 34:19, KJV).

Bullet Points to Feed On

- Assassins will often seem as if they have your back, all the while, leaving you wide open to be attacked.

- Assassins form allegiances with those inside of your camp to gain vital information on how, when and where they will attack you.

- Assassins will employ decoys to remain undetected while sending hidden hits against you. Watch the company you keep and the people you connect with.

It's of great importance to put on the full armor of God every day and pray for a blood hedge of protection against these spiritual snipers assigned to kill you spiritually, mentally and emotionally. If you remain suppressed and oppressed in the spirit, you will become blind to the enemy's tactics, rendering you too weak to fight. Pray about every connection in your life and don't count it strange when someone shows up simply just to help you fight, such as in my case. There were some mighty warriors of God who connected with me in that season of my life, and their assignments were to simply help me fight. After the battle was over and I recovered from the embarrassment, I realized that I had laid out too much information for the enemy to use to bind me.

The worst battle is within you. After the truth manifests and the debris clears, you will find peace. The reality of this situation is the person the enemy used to bind me was someone I would have never been attracted to in my sound mind. He wasn't my type, but that serpent, the devil, dressed that chameleon up to look like what I had been praying for. The enemy is crafty; he will study you until he has enough insight into you to devour you, but just know this: "*The joy of the Lord is your strength*" (Nehemiah 8:10).

I dare you to get in His presence and stay there until strategic instructions come. God will never allow His children to be overtaken by the enemy. He will provide a way of escape and He will rescue you.

"The LORD shall go forth as a mighty man, he shall stir up jealousy like a man of war: he shall

cry, yea, roar; he shall prevail against his enemies" (Isaiah42:13).

He is (Jehovah Gibbor). Jehovah Gibbor is the God who defends; the Man of war.

Empowerment Missiles

- If you have found yourself in this type of situation, seek the Lord and pray for reinforcement to assist you with your battle plan.

- Don't rehearse it. Allow God to renew your mind, and this forgiveness begins with you forgiving yourself. Find encouraging scriptures to apply to your wounds until you are healed.

- Perform a spiritual housecleaning in every room, area, and space that the Holy Spirit has brought to your attention. Anoint your home and re-dedicate it to the Lord.

- Remove contaminated items. Invest in a new bed, sheets and comforter. Never lay in toxic waste as it will pollute your mind and spirit.

Reflection Questions

- What signs do you believe God will show you if you are involved with a counterfeit?

- Have you had any dreams that you feel were warnings?

- Did your courtship seem like a fairy tale?

- Did your family and friends warn you or continue to tell you to be careful?

- After you have introspected, what have you learned from this experience?

- What did the end the journey teach you about waiting on God?

- What did the end of journey teach you about yourself?

Chapter 5

Love Homework: Signs of a Wounded Woman

I thought that time healed all wounds. I have to say that this is not necessarily true. There are many people walking around with unhealed wounds. When we are broken and wounded, our mindsets are cloudy and our decisions, most of the time, are predicated from this wounded stream. A fragmented spirit is a spirit that cannot function wholly. Many times when our spirits are broken, we deal with those involved with us in pieces. If we receive a piece of something, we are not receiving the fullness of it. For example, a person who is already broken in spirit, mind and emotions will not be able to comprehend the depths of wholeness. Many times, brokenness is the culprit behind abusive relationships. Someone did not allow God to heal those broken pieces and restore them before moving on to the next relationship. A wounded woman is even more unstable, and if she does not receive healing and restoration, she will remain broken.

It is a tragedy to see a woman be violated, not just physically, but spiritually. Most of the time, this violation is a casualty within itself, and for those who admire her from afar, it's heart-wrenching. Amnon and Tamar were both King David's children, but they had different mothers. Amnon became overwhelmingly obsessed with his sister's beauty that he plotted to have her. Innocent and naive, Tamar fell into his trap and was raped. Amnon violated Tamar in more ways than just stealing her virtue (innocence). He robbed her of her essence and future. Tamar's essence (core, substance, and soul) became fragmented. King

Love Homework: Signs of a Wounded Woman

David had to deal with betrayal once again as it played out within his family. His son repeated the same cycle of deception, murder, and mayhem that he had done in his early years. Even though David had repented of his foulness, it still remained in his bloodline. His own daughter's soul was ripped through rape at the hands of his son, Amnon. The most crucial blows to one's soul is when the wound is inflicted by someone with an inside connection to you. This caused Tamar to hide herself, never to be restored from such trauma, even after Absalom (her full brother) murdered Amnon. There are many Tamar's walking around presently without any outward signs of trauma, but internally, they are bleeding profusely. They continue to bandage those wounds in a cycle of toxic relationships. Many have become immune to being hurt, and they accept being mistreated because it's normal to them. A wounded woman will always take the low road out of fear of being exposed and having her wounds pointed out. A wounded woman does not ask many questions. There is a cause and effect for the unauthorized relationships we involve ourselves in. When a wounded woman does not pray about the man she's dating, she falls victim to false expectations, and this sets her up to ride an unplanned emotional roller coaster. Broken women continue to commit forgery by wrapping themselves up in people not equipped to heal the fragmented pieces of their lives. Wounded women gravitate towards men with controlling spirits disguised as concern and love. Control is a subtle form of abuse because the victim thinks it is genuine concern and care on the part of their pursuer, but in reality, it is a tactic of the abuser to mask the abuser's true motive.

An abuser preys on women who are deficient in some areas in their lives. Many times, his prey is a woman with a faulty father /daughter relationship or a woman who grew up in a dysfunctional environment where it was the norm for males to control and abuse her. An abuser's prey is usually a woman who feels she has never been validated; therefore, her worth is unknown.

Many times, victims of abuse have cut off all communication with their family members, friends and anyone who displayed any concern for their well-being. Verbal insults, terrorizing, teasing, emotional manipulation and blame are also patterns of emotional abuse that are utilized by the abuser. These tactics are designed to humiliate and chisel away at the victim's esteem.

Emotional abuse is a toxic relationship in itself, therefore, it could be hazardous to an individual's health.

"Be sober, be vigilant; because your adversary

the devil, as a roaring lion, walks about, seeking whom he may devour" (1 Peter 5:8, KJV).

We have to be on high alert against the spirit of control that runs with a counterfeit spirit. Many times, a counterfeit utilizes control to imprison the woman caught in the dance of manipulation, enticement and fantasy.

Chapter 6
Love Homework; Double Trouble

"If I speak in the tongues of men and of angels, but have not love, I am only a resounding gong or a clanging cymbal. If I have the gift of prophecy and can fathom all mysteries and all knowledge, and if I have a faith that can move mountains, but have not love, I am nothing. If I give all I possess to the poor and surrender my body to the flames, but have not love, I gain nothing. Love is patient, love is kind. It does not envy, it does not boast, it is not proud. It is not rude, it is not self-seeking, it is not easily angered, and it keeps no record of wrongs. Love does not delight in evil but rejoices with the truth. It always protects, always trusts, always hopes, and always perseveres. Love never fails. But where there are prophecies,

they will cease; where there are tongues, they will be stilled; where there is knowledge, it will pass away. For we know in part and we prophesy in part, but when perfection comes, the imperfect disappears. When I was a child, I talked like a child; I thought like a child, I reasoned like a child. When I became a man, I put childish ways behind me. Now we see but a poor reflection as in a mirror; then we shall see face to face. Now I know in part; then I shall know fully, even as I am fully known. And now these three remain: faith, hope and love. But the greatest of these is love" (1 Corinthians 13:1-13, NIV).

I gave it to Cameron (my new boyfriend) as plain as I could. We were at a place in our relationship where I had told him repeatedly to do his love homework, because he was reflecting lust, insecurity, lack of trust and a temper imparted by the devil. Cameron did everything he could think of to break me, and the more I cried out, the more he robbed me of my energy and time. There I was again with my heart suspended on the line. Another cycle of looking for love in all the wrong places and faces, when God had been there the entire time... watching me and telling me to come back to Him, my first love. Cameron was my childhood sweetheart and playmate, even before I knew my first husband. Cameron and I had unresolved issues of what should've or could've happened between us. Of course, these red flags should have been seen from a mile away. Later, in the midst of our toxic relationship, I became aware that there was an uncovered soul tie between us. Many of us regress back to those old relationships when we haven't resolved our feelings for the people we once dated. Most times, old feelings resurrect and resurface when we are in our state of vulnerability. I was in a season of my life where I truly wanted to believe that Cameron was the one I'd left behind. His actions showed me that he hadn't fully learned the true definition of love.

When things did not go Cameron's way, he would throw temper tantrums or throw insults at me. He would pick apart at my spirit until I had no fight left in me and no room to holler, scream or cry. Some of our arguments were orchestrated straight from hell, but I was in such a state of self-inflicted guilt and low self-worth after making the mistake of marrying Willis that I punished myself by allowing Cameron to claw at my mind. He did not physically hit me, but with every insult he spoke, I felt as if he'd kicked a hole in my soul. Many times, I believed that Satan himself was supplying Cameron with the ammunition to muzzle me.

Love Homework; Double Trouble

A lot of times, pieces of me lay fragmented all over the floor as I waited for my roller coaster of a relationship to come down. Cameron routinely apologized and promised to get help, but those words became commonplace. I began to recite his speech line by line. I cried out to God, and I asked Him why no man had ever loved me like He's loved me. He began to impart revelation into me about love. There are many people who claim to know love, but as soon as the tides change, their actions override their words. Their love turns into an obsession, and that obsession turns into control. Control steals the innocent, purified love in a person until that person's love begins to wax cold. Not being properly healed from this toxic, life draining relationship does what it was sent out to do. It paralyzes you with the unresolved issues to keep your heart imprisoned with hatred.

One day, as I was praying to the Lord concerning my relationship with Cameron and I asked God again why Cameron's love was so unbalanced. What the Lord revealed to me was shocking, yet very life changing. God shared with me that Cameron had unresolved issues within his childhood caused by his parents' volatile, dysfunctional and abusive relationship. He'd never seen an example of pure love, and he does not know how to recognize it. Plus, he could not possibly love me like he thought he did because he did not and had never been shown a genuine demonstration of a relationship rooted and grounded in Jesus Christ.

God revealed to me that in Cameron's family line, there was a generational curse of failed marriages, no desire to be married, and a strong anti-Christ spirit. When the Lord revealed this to me, I cried, but not so much about what the Lord was speaking to me, but I wept because he did not have God as his foundation. I was absorbing so much insight into the depths of what resided in this broken, fragmented spirit of a man who wrestled with not only himself, but the unconditional love I exemplified and tried to bring into the relationship. That was a "light bulb" moment for me. All of his efforts to show his love for me continued to be outweighed by the repeated cycles of abuse he'd witnessed throughout his family. His examples of love were nothing short of abusive. He felt the need to break me down so he would take control of the situation and build me back up the way he wanted me to be. He would never take responsibility for his own actions.

Some of us can relate to how Satan comes, and with the power of suggestion, begins to play with our feelings. Satan begins to rob us of the plans and purpose of God that

commissioned us to love in the first place.
"A double- minded man is unstable in all his ways" (James1:8, KJV).

If you are not balanced in your love walk with God, how can you slow dance with "the love" sent in the natural? If we continue our intimacy with God and allow Him to lead us, we can love the way He designed us to love. How can you be intimate with a man in the natural when you can't be intimate with God in the spirit? It would be callous if our Lord and Savior changed His love for us just like that. How awful would it be if God withdrew His promises to us as soon as we sinned?

"He has loved us with an everlasting love" (Jeremiah 31:3, KJV).

"The Lord appeared from of old to me [Israel], saying, yes, I have loved you with an everlasting love; therefore with loving-kindness

have I drawn you and continued my faithfulness to you" (Jeremiah 31:3, NLT).

I had to renounce the word curses spoken over my mind, spirit and heart in order to allow God to make new the parts of me that had been damaged by my toxic relationships. I had to release Cameron from my heart and mind, but I do pray that he will humbly allow the Lord to break up the accursed ground within his family lineage, his heart and his spirit.

I was going around in circles; I was dizzy. This was the result of me not dealing with those unresolved issues and hidden curses within my own bloodline. Once I began to do my research (love homework), I was amazed at the family members who were also enslaved to dysfunctional relationships. Within my family dynamics alone, there were many generational curses, strongholds and bondage running rampant. What I discovered while doing my homework was: many of my family members were never married, and didn't have any clue what real commitment, covenant and love was. So, in a sense, my attachments from the past had backgrounds similar to my own background. Some of the people in my family substituted abuse for love, and they have long suffered through many black eyes, lies and affairs. In my first marriage, I'd never suffered a black eye, but my husband had physically attacked me once he'd become tormented by his own guilt and conviction. He was more of a mental, emotional and verbal abuser because he did not want to be labeled a "woman beater". He thought having affairs was normal, because, in his bloodline, adultery was accepted. Both of his parents had outside relationships where other children had been conceived and born.

I told the Lord one night that I wanted Him to sever all the strongholds, curses, and bondage from my family lineage. When I came to the realization that the strongholds, curses, and bondage had to be renounced in my life, I surrendered to God so He could start the refining process.

The Lord spoke to me and said, "I am going to use it all for my glory." Going through refinement was not pretty. As the Lord began to refine me, I found out just how painful the process is. The Lord had me go back into my family's bloodline and denounce any and every strongman that had transferred to me in conception. It was a painful process, but God applied His healing balm to each area of my heart as He began to heal me. In part of the spiritual surgery, God allowed me to feel the depths of the roots being cut out, and He informed me that He was ensuring I would never embrace those strongmen again.

Nowadays, my discernment is sharp, and my spiritual radar will go off whenever I'm in the presence of those familiar strongmen.

If your passions are simply passions between the sheets and there is no substance outside of what you do in the bedroom, chances are, you're in lust, not love. Intimacy is more than bed and sheets; its intimacy (in- to-me-see). Being intimate (into me) entails knowing me from the inside out (my strengths, weaknesses, what moves me, my dislikes, and pains). It means to be truly invested in the assignment. It is important that you are sure that your assigned mate has been conditioned and positioned to fulfill his position in the God appointed, anointed and ordained covenant. Time is something that has no rules or regulations, therefore, mismanaging it by investing it in someone who has not been conditioned, refined and equipped to cover you leaves you open to the attacks of the enemy. God is a redeemer of time, and His grace is sufficient for us, however, we have to learn that when we are unresponsive in our folly, there will be times when He will also be unresponsive to us. Time is precious and we are to utilize it for our purposes in God. The devil knows how to distract and hinder an individual, and he often does this by hijacking time. This is done through unforeseen chaos, including family members and friends being used to interrupt the person who is trying to remain in alignment with God's instruction.

Reflection Questions

- Have you done your love homework?

- Have you broken generational curses assigned to your family to keep you from having a fulfilling relationship with God?

- Have you inquired of your prospective spouse concerning family dynamics, and are there any unresolved generational curses?

- Have you truly sought the Lord for your assigned mate?

- What has this chapter brought out of you?

- Have you renounced toxic relationships?

◆ Are you still connected to people, places and things that cause you to stumble or revisit your relationship with the counterfeits?

Chapter 7
The Company We Keep

A lot of us, including myself, are wrestling with people, places and things that God has already given an eviction notice to in our lives. As a matter of fact, you have wrestled with the verdict, even though He has clearly told you to turn it loose; He's already finished it. I mean God has put to death some things in your life; you just have to turn them loose. Some of us are holding on to dead people, dead places and dead things, and it stinks in God's nostrils. We know God has told us to delete the numbers, erase the conversations and sever the ungodly soul ties. God has orchestrated every detail of the situation in order for us to come out victorious. We must stop looking back and close our ears to unauthorized counsel. Stop the madness of playing ring around the rosy with your destiny because you refuse to confront what God wants you to confront. Some of you are self-destructing. You already know the relationship has been canceled, but you still keep going in the prayer lines and praying for the same thing. Ask God what it is that He has lined up for you. Many of us are coveting another person's position and wasting time posturing ourselves before God, when what we are waiting on is assigned to someone else. Why keep waiting when God says that we should not covet our neighbor's goods? Get before God and detoxify yourself.

Many of you have not moved forward in ministry because some person told you that it was not your time. There is nothing wrong with serving, but you've got to know when God has changed your season. God is El Roi, the God who sees, and He speaks clearly.

"That is right, and it means that I am watching, and I will certainly carry out all my plans" (Jeremiah 1:12, NLT).

Nobody gets away with coming against God's children. The plans of God's heart are eternal. God goes ahead of His people to clear a path for them. We have endured some hard trials, difficult tribulations, pathetic persecutions, and unrighteous judgment, but we are still standing. We don't look like what we been through. Turn it loose; don't wrestle with your problems. God has already judged the situation and served a verdict to it!

"But the Lord's plans stand firm forever; his intentions cannot be shaken. What joy for the nation whose God is the LORD, whose people he has chosen for his own. The LORD looks down from heaven and sees the whole human race. From his throne, he observes all who live

on the earth. He made their hearts, so he understands everything they do. The best-equipped army cannot save a king, nor is great strength enough to save a warrior. Don't count on your warhorse to give you victory -- for all its strength, it cannot save you.

But the LORD watches over those who fear him, those who rely on his unfailing love. He rescues them from death and keeps them alive in times of famine. We depend on the LORD alone to save us. Only he can help us, protecting us like a shield. In him, our hearts rejoice, for we are trusting in his holy name" (Psalm 33:11-21, NLT).

Psalm 33:11-21 should be the assurance you need. God is not confused regarding His plans for your life, and whatever He has to do get His plans to come forth, He will. That is, of course, unless you reject His plans altogether.

Sound the Alarm

Sounding the alarm is to provoke your spiritual house into exposing the things that aren't supposed to be there, things that hide in the cracks and crevices. I challenge you to take inventory of what's hiding within you and release it. WARNING COMES BEFORE DESTRUCTION. God has been speaking to some of us that it is eviction time for those who aren't assigned to our lives. It is even time to stop doing the things we think nobody knows about. God wants it all. This is a service announcement and the alarm has been sounded. As we become more knowledgeable about our purpose and God's plans for our lives, our associations will begin to resemble the stages of growth we're in. The company you keep should also be in alignment with your position and posture in God. Kingdom and carnality do not have anything in common.

When you remain carnal-minded, nothing of the Spirit can be contained in your spirit because the flesh only thinks of itself. The lust of the flesh, lust of the eyes and the pride of life will always birth causalities of war. Lust becomes a casualty when you continue to be enslaved to it. It is called self-inflicted blindness, and the Lord is not pleased when we fail to utilize the tools He has put before us. After all, these tools were designed to help us overcome sin in every area of our lives. Not only do we need to renew our minds, but we need to allow God to transform us in every area of our lives.

Prayer develops intimacy between you and God. When you pray to God, He will deposit strategies in you that will be effective in fighting the enemy and his schemes against you. When we remain ignorant to the plots, plans and diabolical spirits assigned to abort the destiny of God on our lives, we give our victories to the enemy. Counterfeit relationships do not excuse us from fulfilling our God-assigned purposes in life. Instead, they will only frustrate us as we continue to feel the tugging of the Holy Spirit, all the while, suffering through sleepless nights and demonic attacks. We must lock the doors and windows within our souls to keep the enemy out. I plead with you to introspect and spend some time with God. Sometimes, allowing the phone to go to voice mail, committing to stay off social media for a while, and truly allowing God to refine, restore and revive you brings fresh oil. The blindness will leave as God removes the spiritual cataracts from your eyes. Many times, we do not allow God to fully refine us and show us when we are in the company of dangerous people. We ignore the signs and symptoms going off in our spirit to cease all interactions and involvement with those people.

The Company We Keep

Sometimes, the company we keep would never have found positions in our lives if we would have done background checks. Background checks are performed before a person is appointed for the position. Character and performance are reviewed before any job offer is made. What is presented is not always genuine. The person who has the spirit of a chameleon can position themselves as if they are everything you need, however it's to divert you from the person's true colors. There are many types of chameleons that have infiltrated and positioned themselves in the lives of God's people. This spirit is so crafty, it can disguise itself as the perfect mate, saying all the right things until it gains your trust and approval. Once full access is given to the chameleon spirit, it begins to adjust itself to prepare to attack its prey. Not all jobs have a ninety day probationary period; some have extended it to six months.

Dangerous company does not need a front row seat into your life to pass inside information to the father of destruction (Satan), and when we do not pray about the company we keep, we become prey. We must ask the Lord to deliver us from wrongful thinking and from remaining in the company of people who have no vision. Many times, we become corrupt by "rear-view mentality", always looking back and never surrendering ourselves to fully move forth in the things of God. The biggest insight that we can grasp is that we, ourselves, are spiritual chameleons, allowing others to mold, adjust and pull us in the direction they want us to go. To some of us, this is a safe place and posture to accept.

"Let us thank the Lord, who has not let our enemies destroy us. We have escaped like a bird from a hunter's trap; the trap is broken, and we are free! Our help comes from the Lord, who

made heaven and earth" (Psalms 124:6-8, GNT).

The Lord wants us to escape the snares and traps of the enemy. Even within our families, we are like prey to family members who feel entitled to whatever our success brings. Those family members observe from the sidelines and they surface just when they sense a major breakthrough coming into our lives. There are those spouses who are sent to offset the blessings of God or to hold up some of our blessings from being birthed. Many women are with men who God did not authorize for their lives. Their bloodlines may be tainted beyond repair and too tainted for a seed from the Lord to come through. Situations like this call for a midnight experience in the presence of God to receive instructions.

Prayer of Discernment to Recognize a Counterfeit

Heavenly Father, I humbly come to you with praise and I glorify Your name, for You are worthy of all the praise. Father, I come to You with a surrendered heart, asking that You protect my mind, body and spirit from the spirit of counterfeit. I ask that You increase my discernment so I may recognize and detect when this spirit is in my presence. Create in me a clean heart and make new the heart that beats within me. Restore my appetite towards the things of God. Make new my associations to reflect Your posture. Make new my time, redeeming it from the hands of the enemy that I may fulfill my purpose and destiny in You. Father God, continuously usher me into your presence that I may remain sensitive to Your leading, instruction and plans. Father God, cover me in your spiritual armor that I may be protected from the attacks of the enemy.

Father, I ask that You honor this prayer in Jesus Name.

Chapter 8
In the Ninth Hour

"From the sixth hour until the ninth hour darkness came over all the land. About the ninth hour, Jesus cried out in a loud voice, Eloi, Eloi," "lama" "sabachthani?"--which means, "My God, my God, why have you forsaken me?" (Matthew 27:45-46, NIV).

Many times, we come to a crossroad in our lives where we cry out, "My God, my God! Why have You forsaken me?" Nothing remotely compares to the agony and anguishes our Lord and Savior Jesus Christ felt on that cross. We all have endured some situations that rocked us to the core of our being, yet and still, God showed up in the ninth hour, just as He'd done for His Son. There are some situations I put myself in that I know should have went a different way, but God intervened. The relationships and the forfeited opportunities caused brokenness within my spirit, and that brokenness forced me to go before God. There were career opportunities that I mishandled without consulting God, and there were many job opportunities I allowed to pass me by because I was caught up in distracting situations. Then, there were those jobs that came easily, but I remained underpaid and unfulfilled. Many of us can relate to being in a position and grateful for the opportunity, but continue to go home day after day feeling unfulfilled. When we do not allow God to lead and guide us, we will continue to have situations that cause God to move in the ninth hour of our anguish. Some experiences are created to draw us closer to God as well as expose the enemy. God will give us strategies to draw Him into our situations. Consider the case of Hannah, who was ridiculed, irritated, and mocked by her husband, Elkanah's other wife, Penninah. Penninah had been fruitful and bore ten children for her husband. Hannah, on the other hand, was barren. Hannah became so radical in her intercession before the Lord that the priest thought she was drunk with wine. In the ninth hour of her heart's cry before the Lord, the priest, Eli, told Hannah to simmer down. We know that at our points of desperation, we can appear drunk to others who do not know the depths of our circumstances. In the ninth hour, after the priest received clarity of Hannah's issue, he granted her petition and told her to go in peace. Hannah made a vow to the Lord that if He blessed her with a son, she would dedicate him back to the Lord. Sometimes, God simply wants to know where He fits in and what He will receive from the ordeal. Sometimes, God simply wants praise, and other times, He wants to know that He will be exalted. Hannah wanted to be fruitful, and in the ninth hour, the Lord remembered Hannah's vow and opened her womb to conceive a son. Hannah named her son Samuel, which translates to "he is from God."

Barren woman, would you posture yourself as Hannah and cry out to the Lord to make you fruitful? Fruitful woman, would you cry out to the Lord that you remain fruitful?

Repentance is something many take lightly, but God takes seriously.

"For the LORD God is a sun and shield: the LORD will give grace and glory: no good thing will he withhold from them that walk uprightly" (Psalms 84:11, ESV).

God longs to give blessings and favor to His children. When we try to move outside of God's timing, our blessings get held up. God's timing is not our timing, for He knows when, how and where He will deposit the seeds of fruitfulness within our lives.

A Defining Moment Nugget

The defining moment is between desperation and destiny; it is when God answers your heart's plea in the ninth hour and when things appear to be barren. This gives God the opportunity to speak to the womb of promise and breathe life into His promises for us, creating an atmosphere for conception.

To my sisters who are yet waiting on your womb to manifest the promises of a natural birth: Get into an intimate place before the Lord and watch the fruit of your womb become blessed. In the ninth hour, the Lord will rescue, restore and refresh you.

To my sisters who are waiting on a husband: Be of good cheer and be comforted in knowing

God knows the exact time of his arrival for your assigned mate. There have been too many self-appointed spouses that a lot of predestined promises just never was able to be manifested. Single women, it is such a gift to be able to have no other concerns to contend with but what the Lord desires of you and from you. The blessings of the Lord are great, and when you are in right alignment to receive them, He releases them faithfully.

Married women: Don't take for granted the positions you hold as wives. It's a ministry that has to nurtured in order for it to be pleasing in the Lord's sight.

Chapter 9
__Through the Fire__

Through the fire and the rain, I have endured so much heartache and pain…
Some situations were self-inflicted, due to the past traumas that were never evicted…
I became consumed in the fire, I became ablaze as I cried out to God to please take away this flame…
As the rain splatters, I hear the Lord say I am here my daughter to heal your heart's matters…
A broken instrument I am before thee…
I pray to the Lord to keep me from ever experiencing some situations again, Lord, hear my plea…
Gently, the Lord speaks to me and says, "My

dear child, there is nothing new under the sun, the situations you have endured have been ordained to refine you and have not just begun...

Sever the ties, and denounce the lies that are tormenting your mind. You are my jewel and I the Lord has been with you through the fire...
~The End

Fire is represented throughout the Bible, and its powerful existence has been symbolic to the Holy Spirit of God. The Bible tells us, "For our God is a consuming fire" (Hebrews 12:29, KJV).

God allows many fire experiences to refine us to become more like Him. Being refined in the fire of God produces a finely tuned instrument, cultivated for the Master's use. When refinement happens, it produces oil in you that pours forth into the lives of those assigned to receive. Being in the furnace of God brings about a surrendered heart, mind and spirit to operate in excellence. Many times, we become so in sync with God that we give no attention to those who are upset that their attempts to destroy us are ineffective. When God centers you in the midst of the fire, He allows everything on you to burn up, including those who have conspired and been hired to kill you. God will never allow His child to be subdued by the evil intentions of man. The Lord warns, *"Stop trusting in man, who has but a breath in his nostrils. Of what account is he?"(Isaiah 2:22, NIV)*

This brings to my remembrance the story of Daniel in the lion's den. Daniel was known to have the spirit of excellence. He excelled in his work, attitude and life, and this made him a target to be attacked. Many of us can relate to Daniel, especially him being lied on, even though the evidence against him was falsified. Sometimes, those who are around us conspire, conceive and initiate judgment against us in order to attack our character, posture and truth in God. Daniel had no errors or faults in him because he was faithful to God. So, the governors, counselors and advisers plotted together to establish a royal statute and create a law that they knew would allow them to arrest Daniel. Look at how strategic these spirits of sabotage arranged to get Daniel thrown in the lion's den. I have learned folks do not have to like each other, but they will form an allegiance to get you if you are on their hit list.

This is how the enemy works in the kingdom of God to break down God's chosen vessels. The enemy will stop at nothing to get God's children to denounce God's power in their lives by creating situations designed to bring them to their knees. This is an "in the fire" experience, and what you do in the fire determines how you come out of it. Some of us remain on our knees, praying and crying out to God, while some of us praise our way through the fire, getting God's attention in the midst of our situations.

Our faithfulness to God causes us to remain on the hit list of Satan, and he devises plan after plan to weaken us. The power of God is far greater than any devil rising up. We must never relinquish our loyalty to God, even in the midst of men-pleasers and those who appear to have the authority to hire, fire, break and make our lives miserable. We must continue to give God praise and thanksgiving, just as Daniel had done. Daniel did not let the decree change his actions one way or another. He did not miss a moment in the presence of "his God", and he endured in the lion's den.

In summary, even the king knew that God

would deliver Daniel from the lion's den. The king spoke, saying to Daniel, "Your God, whom you serve continually, He will deliver you." The king was troubled in his spirit by what he commanded to be done to Daniel, but because of pride, he threw Daniel into the lion's den. In secret, the king turned down his own plate and couldn't sleep because of this situation. How many of us know that there are many who are in the midst of our accusers, and they know the truth about us, but because of pride, they refuse to speak up for us? How many of us know people who witness the judgments cast upon us, and will go into the secret place and pray on our behalves that the truth will be exposed? How many of us know people who stand on the sidelines watching us go through the fire, but refuse to intervene? Within the body of Christ, we have encountered those who were in position to shift our circumstances, but refused to surrender to the leading of the

Holy Spirit. In the body of Christ, there are many who have an overabundance of supplies, but refuse to help. Daniel's enemies were encamped all about him and pressured the king to judge and condemn Daniel. This is how many will come up against an individual who's in the fire. God sent His angels to shut the lion's mouth, and He will send them on our behalves too.

Refuse to relinquish your kingdom authority in God and continue to praise all the more. Praise is a weapon that confuses the enemy. Top your praise off with worship and watch God come and sit with you right in the midst of the trial. Praise and worship moves God beyond our scope of understanding. I have endured situations, from broken marriages to assigned bounty hunters hired to kill the destiny within me. I admit, there were some attacks that tore me down, but the Lord sent assigned women and men of God to build me back up.

One day, the Lord told me, "There is a difference between being a man and woman of God and being in God." The Lord said that many in the body of Christ are from Him, but the definition of being called a man or woman of God has been misrepresented. There are many who hide behind religious titles, but their agenda is not of God. Many have committed treason in the spirit and against the kingdom of God. The Lord told me to remain sensitive to His voice, and He will tell me who is of God and who is in God. When you are in the fire, you learn insight beyond your own natural comprehension. The Holy Spirit begins to deposit in depth revelation from the Throne Room into your spirit to keep you standing in the fire. In the fire, there will be some instances when the Lord Himself will position you to lay low and allow the kingdom of Heaven to go to battle. These are the times when God will cause you to rest in Him, and He may reveal things to you through dreams, visions or in His Word.

For those who do not know the story of Daniel in the lion's den, Daniel's accusers were judged and condemned and given the same sentence they gave to Daniel, and they were eaten by the lions. This is spiritual warfare in action. The traps and plots of the enemy were returned to the senders. When the kingdom shows up, there is not a demon in hell that can stand up against its power. We must stand firm on our beliefs, faith and trust in God to know that He will bring the kingdom of Heaven to fight for us. The fire represents so much in our lives, and it reveals to those who question its presence in our lives just how strong it really is. When we need to speak to the Lord, He has given us tongues of fire that cannot be interpreted by man or Satan. Our heavenly language is designed for us to make intercession to the Father without interruption. Our intercession causes God to strategically plan for an ambush on the enemy's camp and take back everything that was stolen from us. We will prosper, persevere and be positioned through the fire.

"And I will put this third into the fire, and refine them as one refines silver, and test them as gold is tested. They will call upon my name, and I will answer them. I will say, 'They are my people'; and they will say, 'The LORD is my God" (Zechariah 13:9, ESV).

Refinement happens in the fire and it draws us closer to the Lord. Many are assigned and positioned to be in the midst of our fiery trials, and they have to announce to others how we are handling our fires. Some are postured to stand guard to make sure that we remain in the fire and report when the coals die down. Some are spectators, watching along the sidelines to see the finality of our situations. Whatever the part an individual is assigned to play, know that God has the final say and has never lost a case. When true repentance with a surrendered heart to God comes, Victorious Overcomer will be your new name. Being redeemed in Christ has full benefits, and it comes with full protection through the fire.

Through the Fire Nuggets

"Be strong and courageous. Do not be afraid or terrified because of them, for the LORD your God goes with you; he will never leave you nor forsake you"(Deuteronomy 31:6, NIV).

"The LORD shall fight for you, and ye shall hold your peace" (Exodus 14:14, KJV).

"For I know the plans I have for you," declares the LORD, "plans to prosper you and not to harm you, plans to give you hope and a future. Then you will call upon me and come and pray to me, and I will listen to you. You will seek me and find me when you seek me with all your heart" (Jeremiah 29:11-13, NIV).

"But no weapon that is formed against you shall prosper, and every tongue that shall rise against you in judgment you shall show to be in the wrong. This [peace, righteousness, security, triumph over opposition] is the heritage of the servants of the Lord [those in whom the ideal Servant of the Lord is reproduced]; this is the righteousness or the vindication which they obtain from Me [this is that which I impart to them as their justification], says the Lord" (Isaiah 54:17, AMP).

"The LORD hath appeared of old unto me, saying, Yea, I have loved thee with an everlasting love: therefore with loving-kindness have I drawn thee" (Jeremiah 33:3, KJV).

This is just a fraction of "in the fire nuggets", and as we go through the fire, God deposits more in us. We must develop confidence that, in Jesus Christ, the fight is always fixed. We must learn to remain sensitive to the voice of God to hear His strategic plans against the enemy. If we obey His instructions, we will not be defeated, nor will we perish in the fire. We will embrace the fire as opportunities that produce access to new realms in the spirit.

www.ingramcontent.com/pod-product-compliance
Lightning Source LLC
Chambersburg PA
CBHW070509100426
42743CB00010B/1795